T0195635

Cursive Writing

Reference Workbook

Doreen S. Castillio

authorHOUSE

AuthorHouse™
1663 Liberty Drive
Bloomington, IN 47403
www.authorhouse.com
Phone: 833-262-8899

Published by AuthorHouse 04/12/2022

ISBN: 978-1-6655-3544-1 (sc)
ISBN: 978-1-6655-3550-2 (e)

SECTION ONE

Lowercase Letters & Uppercase Letters

top line

middle line

bottom line

below the bottom line

/// slant

cursive starts with c

space 1

space 2

space 3

tail

smiley face

short letters

tall letters

below the bottom line letters

a c i i m n o r s w w x ß

b d h k l t

PREVIEW

g j p q y z

f

A B C D E F G H K L M N

O P Q R S T U V W X

f y z

c c   g g

a a

ROUND LETTERS

o ö   q q

d d

c

a

o

d

g

q

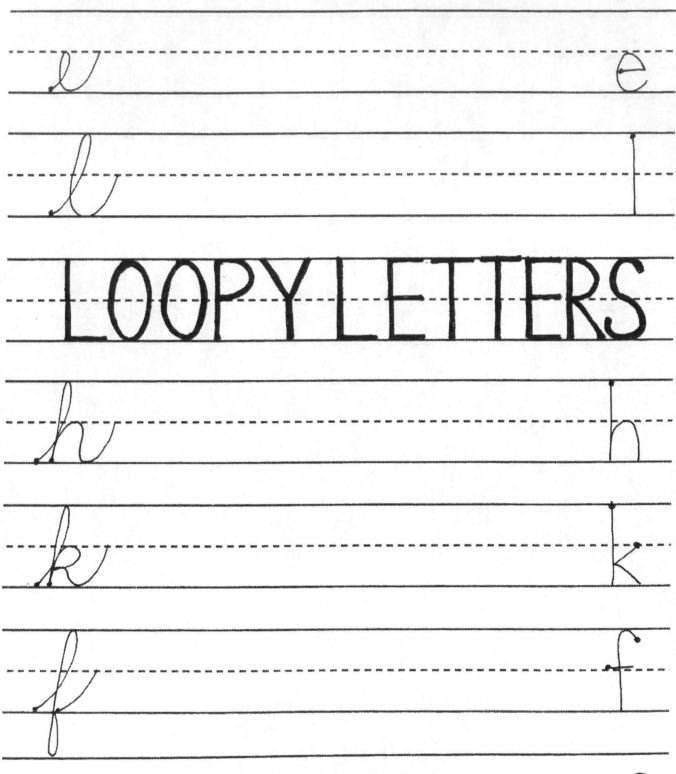

LOOPY LETTERS

Samples

e

fat

no space

open

l

too straight

cross here

h

too wide

retrace no space

no

no

k

even

too far down; no bump

bump too high

f

use a slanted line to guide letter

Try Try Again!

b b

o o   r v

SMILEY FACES

Don't touch bottom
no no

v n   w w

w w

7

8

n m   v v

m m m   x x

BUMPY LETTERS

h h   y y

z z

m   *y*

m

h

n n

n n

n ny

10

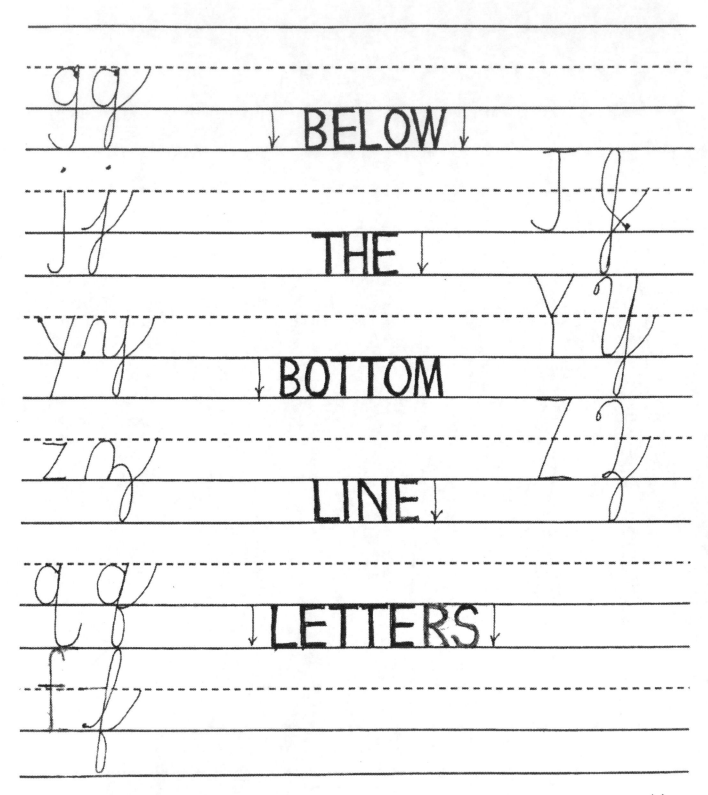

BELOW

THE

BOTTOM

LINE

LETTERS

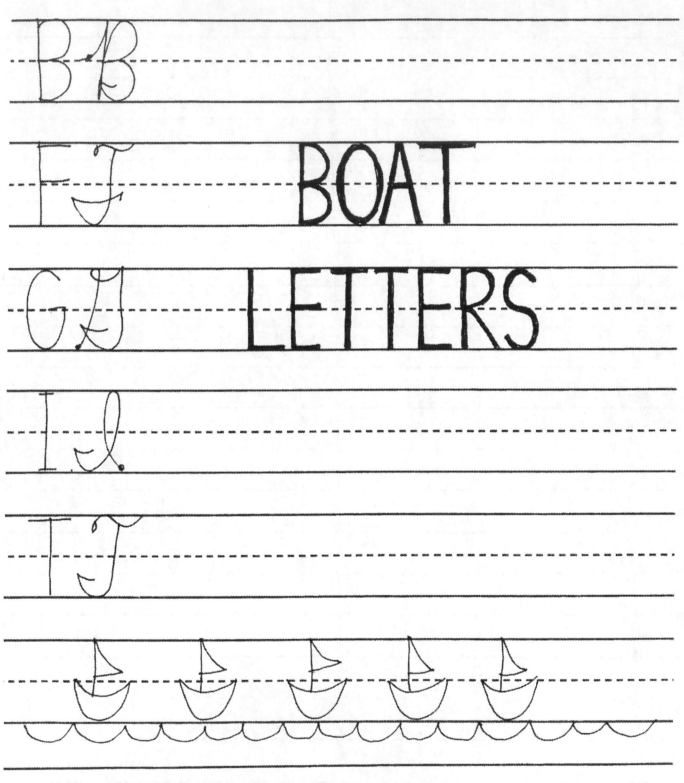

BOAT

LETTERS

13

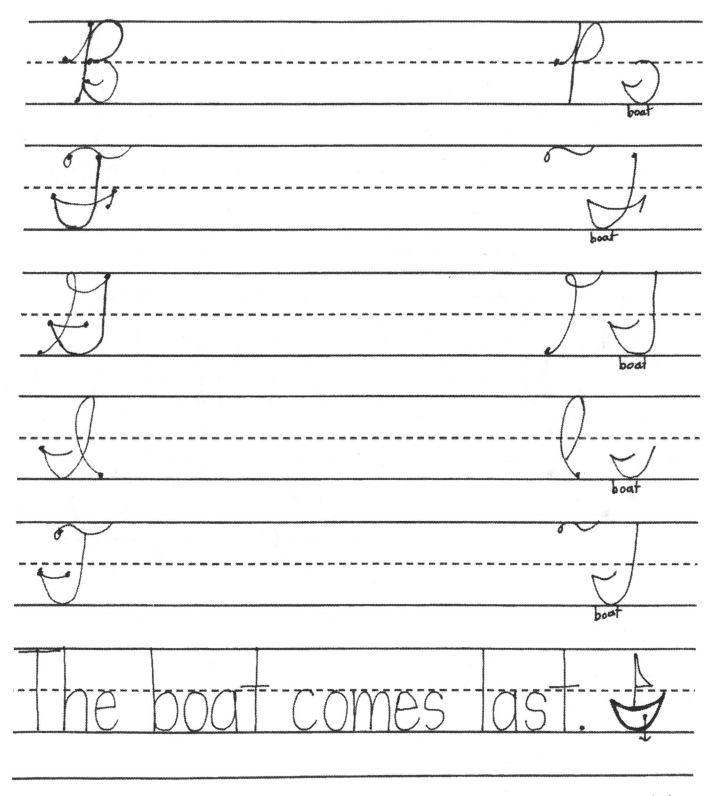

boat

boat

boat

boat

boat

The boat comes last.

14

MORE CAPITALS

NO LOOP

NO LOOP

MORE

Start the Same

CANDY CANE LETTERS

YOU DECIDE

WITH LOOP?

WITHOUT LOOP?

18

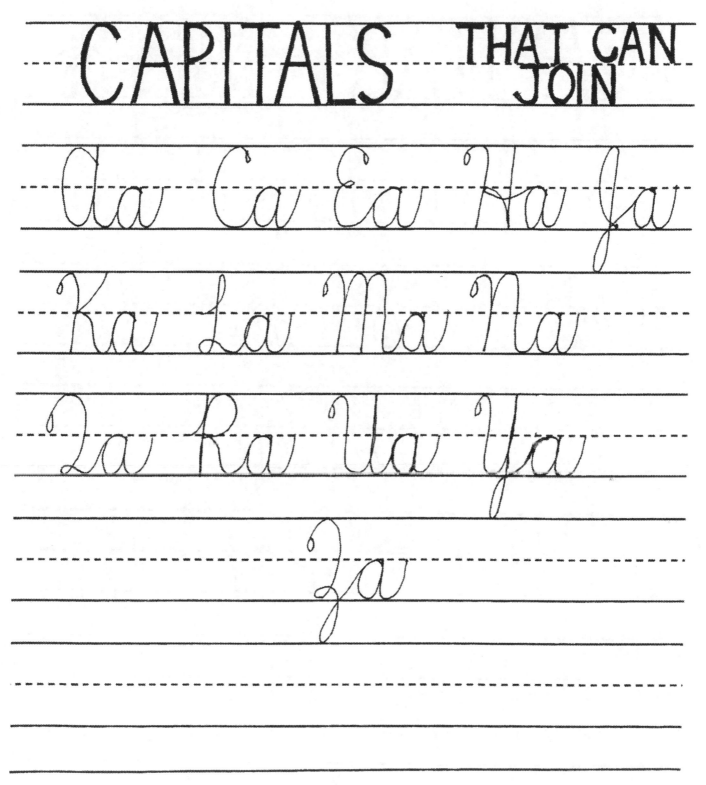

CAPITALS THAT CAN JOIN

Aa Ca Ea Ha Ja

Ka La Ma Na

Qa Ra Ua Ya

Za

CAPITALS THAT DO NOT JOIN

Ba Da Fa Ga La

Oa Pa Sa Ta Va

Wa Xa

SECTION TWO

Letter Joining

a+a aa a+b ab a+c ac

LETTER JOININGS

Add EACH letter

to EVERY letter.

...z+x zx z+y zy z+z zz.

Get lined paper 1st.

aa ab ac ad ae af ag ah

ai aj ak al am an ao ap

aq ar as at au av aw

ax ay az

ba bb bc bd be bf bg

bh bi bj bk bl bm bn

bo bp bq br bs bt bu

bv bw bx by bz

ca cb cc cd ce cf cg

ch ci cj ck cl cm cn

co cp cq cr cs ct cu

cv cw cx cy cz

da db dc dd de df dg

dh di dj dk dl dm dn

do dp dq dr ds dt du

dv dw dx dy dz

ea eb ec ed ee ef eg eh

ei ej ek el em en eo

ep eq er es et eu ev

ew ex ey ez

fa fb fc fd fe ff fg

fh fi fj fk fl fm fn

fo fp fq fr fs ft fu

fv fw fx fy fz

ga gb gc gd ge gf gg

gh gi gj gk gl gm gn

go gp gq gr gs gt gu

gv gw gx gy gz

ha hb hc hd he hf hg

hh hi hj hk hl hm hn

ho hp hq hr hs ht hu

hv hw hx hy hz

ia ib ic id ie if ig ih

ii ij ik il im in io ip

iq ir is it iu iv iw ix

iy iz

23

ja jb jc jd je jf jg jh

ji jj jk jl jm jn jo

jp jq jr js jt ju jv

jw jx jy jz

ka kb kc kd ke kf kg

kh ki kj kk kl km kn

ko kp kq kr ks kt ku

kv kw kx ky kz

la lb lc ld le lf lg lh

li lj lk ll lm ln lo

lp lq lr ls lt lu lv lw

lx ly lz

24

ma mb mc md me mf

mg mh mi mj mk ml mm

mn mo mp mq mr ms mt

mu mv mw mx my mz

na nb nc nd ne nf ng

nh ni nj nk nl nm nn

no np nq nr ns nt nu

nv nw nx ny nz

oa ob oc od oe of og oh

oi oj ok ol om on oo op

oq or os ot ou ov ow

ox oy oz

25

pa pb pc pd pe pf pg

ph pi pj pk pl pm pn

po pp pq pr ps pt pu

pv pw px py pz

qa qb qc qd qe qf qg

qh qi qj qk ql qm qn

qo qp qq qr qs qt qu

qv qw qx qy qz

ra rb rc rd re rf rg

rh ri rj rk rl rm rn

ro rp rq rv rs rt ru

rv rw rx ry rz

sa sb sc sd se sf sg

sh si sj sk sl sm sn

so sp sq sr ss st su

sv sw sx sy sz

ta tb tc td te tf tg

th ti tj tk tl tm tn

to tp tq tr ts tt tu

tv tw tx ty tz

ua ub uc ud ue uf ug

uh ui uj uk ul um un

uo up uq ur us ut uu

uv uw ux uy uz

va vb vc vd ve vf vg

vh vi vj vk vl vm vn

vo vp vq vr vs vt vw

vv vw vx vy vz

wa wb wc wd we wf wg

wh wi wj wk wl wm wn

wo wp wq wr ws wt wuwv

ww wx wy wz

xa xb xc xd xe xf xg

xh xi xj xk xl xm xn

xo xp xq xr xs xt xw

xv xw xx xy xz

ya yb yc yd ye yf yg

yh yi yj yk yl ym yn

yo yp yq yr ys yt yu

yv yw yx yy yz

za zb zc zd ze zf zg

zh zi zj zk zl zm zn

zo zp zq zr zs zt zw

zv zw zx zy zz

29

SECTION THREE

Writing Words

PRACTICE

MAKES

PERFECT

Got lined paper?

Words / Sentences

c a o e t d t words

cat doll toad local

cot eel cocoa total

doodle oat tall odd

dot coal ladle date

late dad lot tattle

Watch joining ☺. Always go up.
☺ do not touch bottom line.

33

c a o e b d t n m h k words

note on neat neat no

mole model mean name

home hot hand hole had

clock meek thank mom

mock math canoe lend

Watch your slant.

34

add u w g q i j words

goat gone town hedge

quack queen wand choke

ouch loud hula we week

quit walk wow watch

uncle it jangle window

Add an extra stroke u u
when u or w begins a word.

35

add r p b f x words

read car red hearing

pink pole place prepare

brag grab beta rabbit

beef fowl fawn feeble

four mix xerox wax box

Now you can read cursive. ☺

36

add y v z s →words

yet buy bye →way bay

your yawn yellow hyena

five over very heaven

eleven favorite travel

zero zoo zebra lizard

soak does some something

Try <u>not</u> to lift up your pen or pencil. ☺

37

SECTION FOUR

Writing Sentences

Aardvarks are awful animals.

Bullies can be big and bad.

Calico cats are so very cute.

Donkeys dive deep in ditches.

Elk and Eel do not eat alike.

Flamingos look just fine.

Gorgeous gorillas are great.

Hungry hyenas like hot dogs.

I love to eat icy, ice cream.

Jumping jacks are just fun.

Kool koalas try to kiss you.

Lions and leopards are lazy.

Monkeys mug and mob mom.

Ninja turtles are not nearby.

Octopi is plural for octopus.

Please promise to propose to me.

Quail run quickly in the quake.

Raccoons rustle up their food.

Snickers are sweet and sugary.

Tortoises swim very slowly.

Ulysses rides on a unicycle.

Violinists play with violins.

Wally went to get wipers.

Xerox my xylophone, please.

Yellow jackets can sting you.

Zillionnaires are zealous people.

Index with loops

a 5	A 16	m 11	M 19
b 9/17	B 15/17	n 11	N 19
c 5	C 16	o 5/9	O 16
d 5	D 16	p 17	P 17
e 6	E 6	q 5/13	Q 20
f 6/13	F 15	r 9/17	R 17
g 5/13	G 15	s 17	S 17
h 6/11	H 19	t 17	T 15/17
i 17	I 15/17	u 3/31	U 20
j 13	J 13	v 9/11 V 19	w 9 W 9/20
k 6	K 19	x 11 X 20	y 11/13 Y 13/20
l 6	L 16	z 13	Z 13

Circle letter when done. ⟲

RECORD SHEET

a c e i m m n o v s w w x 13 ↕
short

b d h k l t 6 ↕
tall

g j p q y z 6 ↕
below↓
the bottom

f ↕
3 spaces ↓

with loops

a B C D E F G H I K L M

N O P Q R S T U V W X 23 ↕
tall

Y Y Z 3 ↕
3 spaces ↓

Copy 2-sided ← Laminate

This book is dedicated to my four children, especially to Patricia Ann "Hauolianela" Cocuzzi who passed away suddenly on February 12, 2019 at the age of 22. "Hauolianela" is Hawaiian for "Happy Angel."

ABOUT THE BOOK

This book was created with the love and desire to perpetuate the teaching and learning of cursive writing. This workbook is for everyone who is wanting and willing to practice and to perfect the art. Letters are grouped by similar shapes like round, loopy, bumpy, smiley, boats, and candy canes. The workbook starts with lowercase and ends with uppercase letters. You'll see a few variations, like candy cane letters. You choose what is more comfortable with or without a loop at the beginning. Practice moves from letters to letters joinings to words to sentences.

ABOUT THE AUTHOR

The author was born in Honolulu, Hawaii. She was educated at Brigham Young University Campus. She earned a Bachelor's Degree in Elementary Education and Associate's Degree in Early Childhood Development. While teaching in Las Vegas, Nevada, Doreen completed two Master's Degree with Lesley University. One degree was in Technology and the other degree was in Creative Arts. Doreen is presently retired in Hawaii. She's the mother of four delightful children and grandmother of six precious grandchildren.

Printed in the United States
by Baker & Taylor Publisher Services